Wild Waves

Lisa Thompson

sundance Newbridge

sundance™ **Newbridge®**

Published by
Sundance Newbridge Publishing
33 Boston Post Road West
Suite 440
Marlborough, MA 01752
800-343-8204
SundanceNewbridge.com

Copyright © text Lisa Thompson
Copyright © illustrations Cliff Watt and Rob Mancini

First published 2002 by
Blake Education, Locked Bag 2022, Glebe 2037, Australia
Exclusive United States Distribution: Sundance Newbridge Publishing

Design by Cliff Watt in association with
Sundance Newbridge Publishing

Wild Waves
ISBN 978-0-7608-6690-0

Photo Credits:
p. 19: Kobal Collection/Warner Bros; p. 25: photolibrary.com;
p. 27 (top): AP/AAP Image/Rick Rycroft; p. 27 (bottom): AP/AAP
Image/Al Grillo; p. 29: Pacific Tsunami Museum Archives,
photographer Cecilio Licos

Printed by Kase Printing, Inc.
Manufactured in Hudson, New Hampshire
March 2019
Kase Job#: 78683
Sundance/Newbridge PO#: 229252

Table
of Contents

Let's Go Surfing Now! 4
Just you and the ocean blue

Waves Gone Wild 14
Up and down—hold on to
your stomach!

The Wildest Waves of All 22
Dangerous and deadly—
batten down the hatches!

Fact File 30

Glossary 31

Index 32

Let's Go Surfing Now!

You see a wave coming towards you. You start paddling—furiously. You feel the wave pick you up. You jump to your feet!

Surfing is one of the most popular sports in the world. Hawaiians have surfed for hundreds of years on the great waves that roll in from the Pacific Ocean. In 1915, Hawaiian Duke Kahanamoku introduced surfboard riding to Australia. Californians also got the surfing bug early in the 20th century. The surf was soon looking crowded!

Surf's Up

Surfers usually prefer big waves to small waves. Big-wave riding is the ultimate test for a surfer. Riding such powerful waves is very dangerous and takes skill and courage. If the waves are very strong and far out at sea, surfers are sometimes towed out to them on jet skis.

Hawaii has some of the biggest waves in the world. The entire Pacific Ocean seems to be behind each wave that thunders down on the coast at Sunset Beach. Strong winds and currents increase the danger. At Waimea Bay, massive waves up to 6 meters (20 ft.) high hit the coast. Until the 1950s, no one dared to surf there. And in the early years of surfing at Waimea Bay, there was just one aim—to survive!

THUNDERING WAVES are perfect for surf competitions.

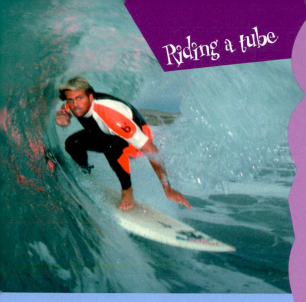

Riding a tube

TALKING SURF!

Clucked: being afraid of the wave

Dropping in: catching a wave that another surfer is on

Dropping in late: catching the steepest part of a wave

Dune: a big wave with peaks

Getting worked: what a wave does to you—like being churned around in a washing machine

Green room: inside a hollow wave, called a tube

Hang ten: hanging ten toes over the front of the board

Puff: a wave that spits

Pumping: a bigger than normal swell

Stuffed: being pushed under the water

Wipe out: falling off

A SURFING GREAT

Duke Kahanamoku was born in Honolulu in 1890. He was one of the greatest surfers ever. In 1925 he rescued eight men when a boat sank off Newport Beach, Australia. He went out and back three times on his surfboard through fierce waves.

Wipe out!

The Perfect Wave

Every surfer has an idea of the perfect wave—one that is big, powerful, hollow, and fast. Surfers look for waves that break consistently from one side to another. Waves that have a good steep and clean break give surfers a long ride with lots of speed and energy.

One of the best surfing thrills is riding inside a steep, hollow wave called a tube. The wave breaks over your head, and you rocket along the face of it. All you can hear is the roar of the wave. It's like a mad race to the end. You have to get out of the wave before it comes crashing down on your head!

How high is that wave?

Surfers around the world have different ways of measuring wave height, but this is generally what they follow.

Small waves: knee to chest height

Medium waves: chest to about an arm's reach over your head

Large waves: a couple of feet overhead to about three times your height

Huge waves: more than three times your height

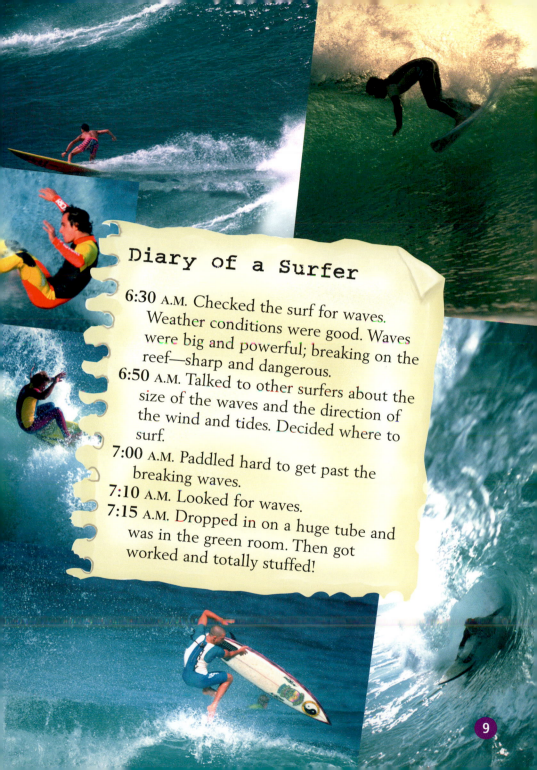

Diary of a Surfer

6:30 A.M. Checked the surf for waves. Weather conditions were good. Waves were big and powerful; breaking on the reef—sharp and dangerous.

6:50 A.M. Talked to other surfers about the size of the waves and the direction of the wind and tides. Decided where to surf.

7:00 A.M. Paddled hard to get past the breaking waves.

7:10 A.M. Looked for waves.

7:15 A.M. Dropped in on a huge tube and was in the green room. Then got worked and totally stuffed!

Wave Speak

Surfers and people who fish know about waves. Their lives depend on recognizing the different types of waves and knowing the power they have.

Most of the waves in the ocean are caused by winds. Wave size depends on the strength of the wind, how long the wind blows, and its **fetch** (the distance it blows). The **Beaufort scale,** shown below, measures wind speed.

The Beaufort Scale

Wind speed (in knots) 1 knot = 1.15 mph	Less than 1 *calm*	1–3 *light air*	4–6 *light breeze*	7–10 *gentle breeze*	11–27 *moderate to strong breeze*
Description	calm sea	ripples on sea	small waves	larger waves	rough sea
Wave height (approx.)	0	0–.30 m (0–12 in.)	0–.30 m (0–12 in.)	0–.30 m (0–12 in.)	.30–4 m (1–13 ft.)

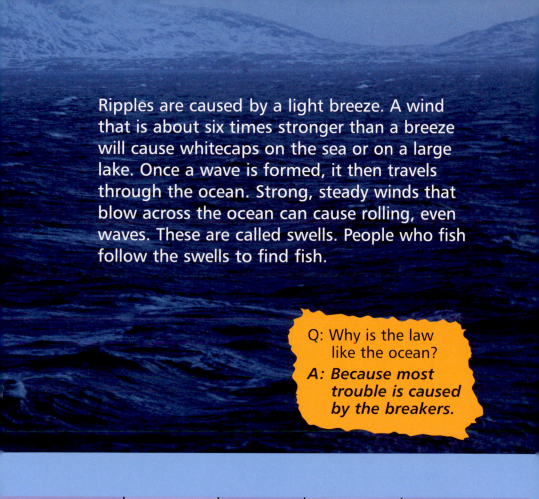

Ripples are caused by a light breeze. A wind that is about six times stronger than a breeze will cause whitecaps on the sea or on a large lake. Once a wave is formed, it then travels through the ocean. Strong, steady winds that blow across the ocean can cause rolling, even waves. These are called swells. People who fish follow the swells to find fish.

Q: Why is the law
like the ocean?

A: *Because most trouble is caused by the breakers.*

28–40 near gale to gale	41–47 strong gale	48-55 storm	56–63 violent storm	64 or greater hurricane
very rough sea	high, rolling sea	very steep waves	mountainous sea	completely raging sea
4–6 m (13–20 ft.)	6 m (20 ft.)	6–9 m (20–30 ft.)	9–14 m (30–45 ft.)	above 14 m (above 45 ft.)

EEK!

Breaking Up

Waves become slower and higher when they reach the shallow water near the shore. As a wave becomes higher, it becomes less stable— like too many dishes stacked one on top of the other. A crash is about to happen!

The Parts of a Wave

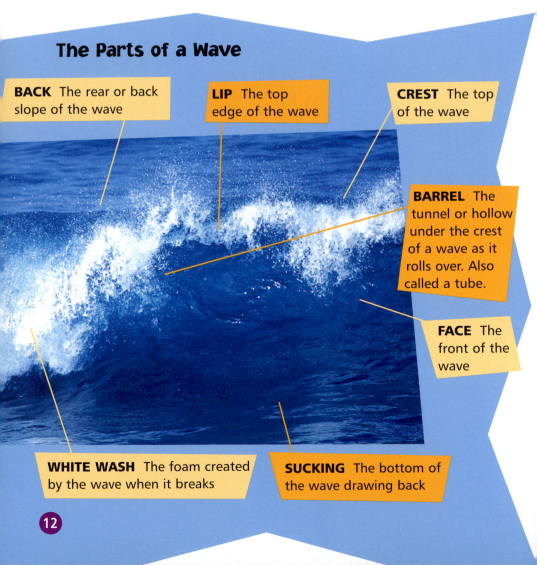

BACK The rear or back slope of the wave

LIP The top edge of the wave

CREST The top of the wave

BARREL The tunnel or hollow under the crest of a wave as it rolls over. Also called a tube.

FACE The front of the wave

WHITE WASH The foam created by the wave when it breaks

SUCKING The bottom of the wave drawing back

Breakers are waves that crash onto the shore. There are three types. The type depends on the slope of the ocean floor at the shore. It also depends on the height of the wave before it reaches shallow water. Spilling breakers occur on beaches with gentle slopes. Plunging breakers happen on beaches where the slope of the beach is steeper. Surging breakers happen on beaches where the slope is very steep. These waves roll up the beach rather than breaking onto it.

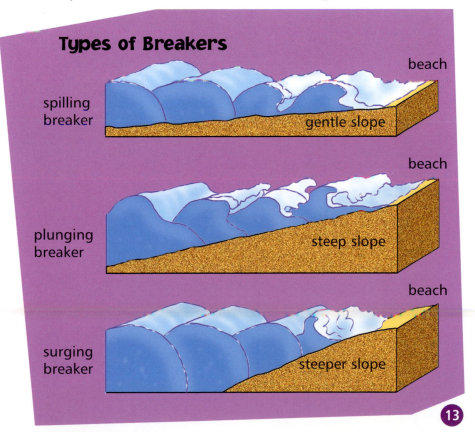

Types of Breakers

beach

spilling breaker

gentle slope

beach

plunging breaker

steep slope

beach

surging breaker

steeper slope

Waves Gone Wild

You're out at sea. The wind is howling. Clouds are rolling in—big, black storm clouds.

Storms at sea can be very fierce. Storm clouds bring strong winds that whip up spray off the ocean. The water piles up in ridges that become waves. As the wind gets stronger, the waves grow bigger and bigger. The sea is soon white with the crests of the waves. Some waves are so wild, they catch everyone off guard.

Danger at Sea

Everyone at sea is in danger when a storm hits. A ship rolls from side to side and up and down like a seesaw in the rough water. Huge waves crash down on the deck, one after the other. They are strong enough to tear open cargo hatches. And then the water will rush in!

Sometimes, strong storm waves slam into a powerful current that is going in the opposite direction. This collision creates freak waves that can be much higher than waves created during a hurricane. Scientists use **radar** images from space **satellites** to chart where and when these deadly waves might occur. Then they warn fishing boats and cruise and cargo ships to change their course—NOW!

WAVES CRASH over a large ship and slam it into a rocky cliff.

Q: What is the best way to survive a shipwreck?

A: *Miss the boat.*

WEATHER SATELLITES help scientists to study weather patterns on a large scale.

The Perfect Storm

Imagine the power of several mighty storms joining together. It's a rare event—so rare that **meteorologists** call it "the perfect storm."

In October 1991, this kind of storm occurred off the coast of Nova Scotia. A high pressure system from the Great Lakes ran into storm winds over an Atlantic sandbar. Then it collided with Hurricane Grace moving north from the Caribbean to create the worst storm of the century. A 70-foot fishing boat called the *Andrea Gail* was in the middle of the storm. The six crewmen faced massive waves in the raging black sea. They radioed the Canadian Coast Guard, but rescue was impossible. The fury of the sea was totally destructive. The *Andrea Gail* and all of its crew were lost in the wild waves.

A SCENE FROM THE MOVIE, *The Perfect Storm* (2000), shows the *Andrea Gail* heading into a huge wave.

The Last Days of the *Andrea Gail*

Canada

Newfoundland

Gulf of
St. Lawrence

The Grand Banks

October 24:
Andrea Gail *begins to head home.*

Nova Scotia

October 28:
The Andrea Gail *radios for the last time.*

October 27:
The boat is in trouble and radios the Canadian Coast Guard.

United
States

19

Disaster Strikes

Hurricanes begin at sea. But the winds, rain, and huge storm waves created by a hurricane can rush onto land with great fury. Storm-surge flooding is the most dangerous part of a hurricane. Pounding waves form dangerous flood currents that sweep through towns, destroying buildings and houses. Nine out of ten people who die in a hurricane actually drown in storm waters.

POWERFUL WINDS swirl around the hurricane's calm center, which is called the eye.

Eye of the hurricane

When a storm surge occurs at the same time as high tide, the flooding is even more dangerous and destructive. For example, in September 1900, more than 6,000 people died at Galveston, Texas, in a hurricane and high-tide storm surge. Many others huddled on the roofs of houses as the water rose around them and the winds roared through the night.

HURRICANE DAMAGE litters the ground.

The Wildest Waves of All

Imagine you are at the beach. Suddenly, the water is sucked away from the sand. You hear a roar. Then you see it—a huge wall of water coming towards you.

It's a **tsunami** (tsoo-NAH-mee)—a series of the biggest waves in the world! Some tsunamis are taller than a 10-story building and many miles wide. In deep water, tsunamis can travel as fast as a jet plane can fly. And when these killer waves reach the shore, they can flatten a city in seconds.

What Is a Tsunami?

A tsunami is a series of giant waves. Most tsunamis occur when an earthquake or a volcano shakes the ocean floor. This creates strong underwater waves. Because the water is so deep, these waves cannot be felt on a boat.

The deeper the water, the faster the tsunami wave travels. But as the wave reaches shallow water near the coast, it slows down. The water behind it begins to pile up. At the same time, the shallow water near the shore is sucked back. The wave swells to between 10 and 30 meters (33–100 ft.) high and hits the shore with terrible force. This wave could be followed by another like it an hour later and then by another. And the first wave may not be the biggest!

A Stone's Throw

To understand how tsunami waves travel, throw a stone into a pool. The stone disturbs the water, just like an earthquake. Bands of ripples travel outward in all directions. They become bigger as they hit the shore. This is exactly how a tsunami moves.

THIS FAMOUS JAPANESE WOODCUT shows an enormous wave towering over Mount Fuji in the distance. A few boats are caught in the stormy waters.

The Meaning of "Tsunami"

Tsunami is a Japanese word. In English it means "harbor wave." Sometimes tsunamis are called tidal waves. But tsunamis have nothing to do with the tides.

津 harbor

波 wave

Causes of Tsunamis

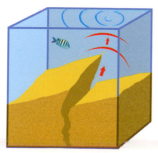

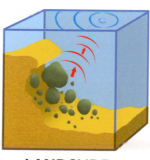

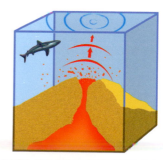

EARTHQUAKE   **LANDSLIDE**   **VOLCANIC ERUPTION**

TSUNAMIS ARE CAUSED by earthquakes, by underwater or other landslides that dump a lot of earth into the ocean, and by underwater volcanic eruptions.

25

Deep Water Alert!

The Pacific Ocean is the world's deepest ocean. Ninety percent of all tsunamis have occurred here because the most dangerous ones usually begin in very deep water. Also, the Pacific has many underwater earthquakes that are caused by movements in the **earth's crust**. Earthquake size is measured on the **Richter scale.**

There are two tsunami warning centers in the world, one in Alaska and the other in Hawaii. Scientists at these centers watch for any **seismic** activity that signals strong earthquakes. Then they warn people on land to go to higher ground away from the coast. They also warn ships in the area not to head for the harbor where the tsunami will hit the hardest. But the system doesn't always work. Seventy-five percent of all tsunami warnings issued since 1948 have been false.

A SCIENTIST CHECKS out the seismic recordings at the Tsunami Center in Palmer, Alaska.

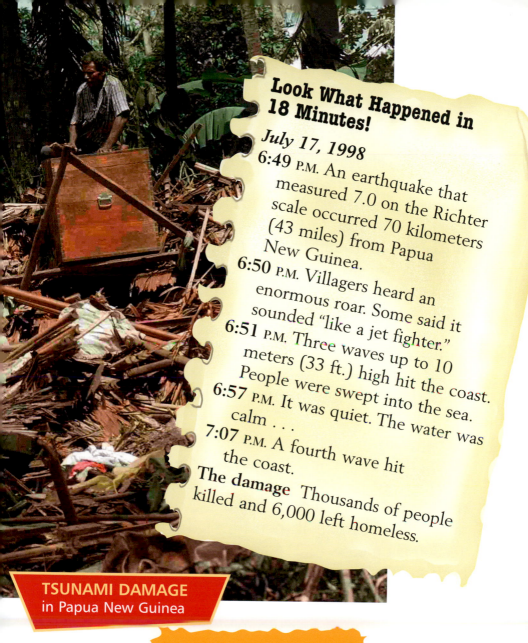

Look What Happened in 18 Minutes!

July 17, 1998

6:49 P.M. An earthquake that measured 7.0 on the Richter scale occurred 70 kilometers (43 miles) from Papua New Guinea.

6:50 P.M. Villagers heard an enormous roar. Some said it sounded "like a jet fighter."

6:51 P.M. Three waves up to 10 meters (33 ft.) high hit the coast. People were swept into the sea.

6:57 P.M. It was quiet. The water was calm . . .

7:07 P.M. A fourth wave hit the coast.

The damage Thousands of people killed and 6,000 left homeless.

TSUNAMI DAMAGE
in Papua New Guinea

Q: Why did the man water half his lawn?

A: *Because the warning center said there was a 50 percent chance of a tsunami!*

Tsunamis Around the World

History is full of the stories of tsunamis. Nearly 7,000 years ago, a tsunami swamped the Shetland Islands, off the coast of Scotland. In 1755, huge waves hit Lisbon, Portugal. About 60,000 people were killed. The deadliest tsunami happened recently, on December 26, 2004. A powerful earthquake in the Indian Ocean generated a tsunami that hit the coasts of Sumatra, Indonesia, Sri Lanka, Thailand, and even eastern Africa. More than 300,000 people were killed.

2004 Indian Ocean: more than 300,000 people died

Tsunamis can travel great distances from where they begin. In 1960, an earthquake off the coast of Chile caused a tsunami that hit the coast of Chile, killing hundreds of people. It then traveled 10,000 kilometers (6,214 miles) to Hilo, Hawaii, causing destruction there.

On April 1, 1946, another tsunami hit Hilo, Hawaii.

Other Disastrous Tsunamis

1946 Aleutian Islands, Alaska: more than 165 people died

1964 Prince William Sound, Alaska: more than 120 people died

1929 Grand Banks, Canada: 29 people died

Pacific Ocean

1998 Papua New Guinea: more than 3,000 people died

1996 Peru: 12 people died

1960 Chilean coast: as many as 2,000 people died

"Watch out, big wave!"

FACT FILE

There is a monster wave that rises in Hawaii when the weather conditions are just right. Surfers call it—*JAWS!*

Tsunamis occur so often in the Hawaiian Islands that maps of tsunami safety zones are printed in the telephone directories.

In 1771, a tsunami hit Ishigaki Island in Japan. It was thought to be about 85 meters (279 ft.) high. That's about as tall as a 25-story building.

In 1996, champion bodyboarder Mike Stewart followed storm waves around the world. He surfed in Tahiti, then Hawaii. Then he flew to California and, finally, Alaska.

The biggest wave ever recorded was 524 meters (1,720 ft.) high. This huge wave struck Lituya Bay on the southern coast of Alaska on July 9, 1958.

GLOSSARY

Beaufort scale a scale that measures wind speed, which affects wave height

earth's crust the outer, solid layer of the earth. Beneath the oceans, the crust is 10 km (6 miles) thick.

fetch the distance the wind blows without changing direction. Fetch affects wave size.

meteorologists people who study the weather and predict weather patterns

radar short for radio detecting and ranging. Radar measures how long the echo of a radio wave takes to come back from an object and the direction of return. This information helps to determine the exact location of an object.

Richter scale a scale that measures the size of an earthquake. Recorded earthquakes have ranged from below zero to about 9 on the scale. Those over 6 are usually dangerous.

satellites devices that orbit the earth. They transmit and record information that is used for communication and research.

seismic relating to or caused by an earthquake

tsunami a series of giant waves

INDEX

Andrea Gail 18–19

breakers 13

earthquakes, underwater 24–26

freak waves 16

Hawaii 5, 6, 26, 28–29, 30

hurricanes 11, 20–21

Kahanamoku, Duke 5, 7

meteorologists 18

Pacific Ocean 5, 6, 26

Perfect Storm, The 18

storms 11, 15–18

surfing 4–10

Stewart, Mike 30

Sunset Beach 6

tsunamis 22–30

tsunami warning centers 26

Waimea Bay 6